The Black Forest
Open-Air-Museum

Vogtsbauernhof

in Gutach

Dr. Dieter Kauß

Willi Sauer
Reinhold Mayer

Edm. von König-Verlag, Heidelberg

Copyright 1986. First edition.

Kunstverlag Edm von König GmbH & Co KG, Heidelberg-Dielheim.
Under contract to Ortenau District Administration
Author: Dr. Dieter Kauß
English Tranlation: Translation Services Dr. Paul Foster
Photographs: Willi Sauer, Ulrich Strauch, Dielheim
                Reinhold Mayer, Ulm
                Page 95 Archive Museum, Vogtsbauernhof
Sketches: Helmut Richter, Herfurt
Layout: Willi Sauer, Ina von König
Aerial photos on pp. 58/59 by kind permission of the Reg. Präsidium in Karlsruhe.

ISBN 3-921 934-44-3

Everything at One Glance

Address:
: Schwarzwälder Freilichtmuseum
,,Vogtsbauernhof''
7611 Gutach, Ortsteil Turm.

Sponsor:
: Ortenaukreis, 7600 Offenburg
Telefon (07 81) 80 55 34

Times of Opening:
: 1st April to 1st November
open daily from 8.30 a.m. to 6 p.m.
Entrance allowed up to 5.30 p.m.

Access:
: A 5 motorway from Karlsruhe or Basle.
Turn off at Offenburg exit and follow B 33
in the direction of Gengenbach, Hausach,
Triberg; after Hausach turn right and
follow signs.

Parking:
: Large parking facilities on the B 33.

Guided tours:
: Possible at any time on application.

On exhibit:
: Forest Museum of the Regional Forestry
Commission, Baden-Württemberg;
Commerce and Handicrafts in the Black
Forest; Regional Costumes; Peasant
Gardens Technical Installations.

Events:
: Special guided tours by arrangement;
Special lectures and seminars;
Special exhibitions.

Information:
: Prospectuses and museum guides in
German, English und French.
Guide to apparatus; Museum library.

Admission:
: By ticket. Discount taken into consideration.

Visitors:
: After 22 years – altogether 7 million;
annually approx. 450 000

That Which is of Interest in Gutach

The Black Forest Open-air Museum, the "Vogtsbauernhof" in Gutach is a fascinating witness to life on the land in this region, its culture and technical achievement and offers a variety of special attractions worth noting.

Many open-air museums in Germany are hard to get at, but Gutach is within easy reach lying as it does on the route between Offenburg and Donaueschingen in the Black Forest. In addition, this route has large parking lots and the visitor can quite easily get to the museum from the B 33 in a few minutes. If our visitor is also a railway enthusiast, he will probably know that the Gutach Museum lies directly on the very well-known Black Forest line. The visitor to the museum simply parks his vehicle in Hausach and then wanders down valley in a straight line through the museum's countryside. This countryside, incidentally, belongs to the most charming of the central Black Forest region. Towards Hornberg, the mountains tower up from narrow valleys while in the Hausach valley direction the landscape broadens. One can still recognize the general outlines of former farm precincts and the way the land was utilized. From these farmsteads a more or less broad strip of land ran straight down the valley partitioned into pasture cultivated land and woodland. Above all, perhaps, it is the houses which strike one most by the way they are constructed and their age. They are original and all go back to the 16th century. For this reason they are also unique and irreplaceable monuments to the skills of house construction in the past as well as a testimony to the way the farming community lived in the different districts of the Black Forest. For the visitor, such houses are not simply isolated buildings removed from their living environment, but can be seen rather as an integral part of today's agricultural scene. For example, one can still see three such houses as displayed at the museum in use today in the Gutach Valley.

In the last analysis, it is the layout of the museum, the view one has of the whole reflecting the outstanding competence of the Museum's initiator, Prof. Hermann Schilli, who set up the houses and fitted them out true to style which evokes our imagination. Finally, the wealth of loving detail which has gone into the house appointments and the flair this demonstrates bestows on the visitors a feeling that here is something special.

The Gutach Museum was opened in 1964 and in the years between 1963 and 1982 continued to be built, fitted out and furnished. It is now complete, but extensions may follow.

View of the Kinzigtäler Speicher at Lorenzenhof.

1 Ticket-Office* / Cash, WC, **2** The „Hotzenwaldhaus", **3** The „Schau-inslandhaus", **4** Kennel*, **5** The Charcoal Pile (Kohlenmeiler), **6** The boundary Stone of St. George's, **7** „Hippenseppenhof", **8** The granary of the High Black Forest, **9** Court Chapel (Hofkapelle), **10** „Vogts-bauernhof", **11** The Gutach granary, **12** The „Zimmerbauernhof"*/ WC, **13** The bakehouse and distillery, **14** The water-powered saw,

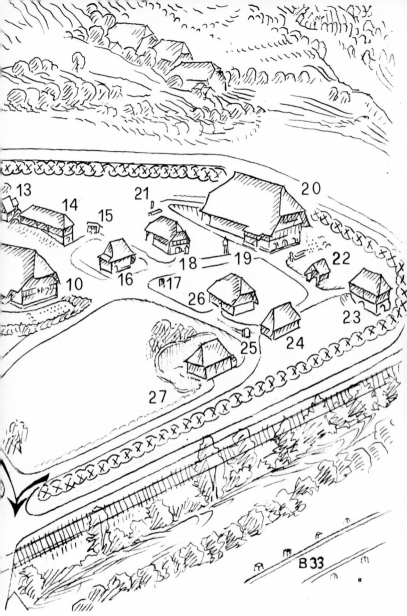

15 The apiary, **16** The mill and the rammer, **17** Württemberg's
boundary stone, **18** The Kinzigtal granary, **19** The Kinzig Valley raft,
20 „Lorenzenhof", **21** The Bähofen stove, **22** The Kinzig Valley
bakehouse, **23** High-performance saw, **24** Hemp-crusher and drying
room, **25** The Falkenstein boundary stone, **26** A peasant's cottage
(Leibgedinghaus), **27** Smithy and oil mill   * closed

The "Hotzenwaldhaus" ②

The Hotzenwald district has flat, rolling hills, is situated high up in the mountains and visited by rough, cold winds. The construction of the house testifies to the kind of climate it was exposed to with its elongated roof on all four sides and a corridor which surrounds both the interior of the house and the stalls. At one end of the house frontage is a projecting, hip-roofed porch approached from ground level by a ramp parallel with the slope of the hill. Its similarity with houses seen in Aargau and also exhibited here cannot be overlooked. The building we see here is an exact replica of the "Klausenhof" house found at Großherrischwand. It goes back

Hotzenwaldhaus showing entrance with its "shield". Right, stalls; left, living area.

to the 18th century and is probably the last Hotzenwald house left standing. From the time the Hotzenwald district was declared a "depressed area" and since has belonged to Baden all the other houses have fallen victim to the axe or have been radically modified. The "Klausenhof" was ear-marked for the Museum at the end of 1978. Accordingly, local authorities decided to keep the house intact within the Hotzenwald itself. The county council (Ortenaukreis) did not then purchase the house in 1979, but

commissioned H. Schilli to erect a replica for the museum which has stood since 1980 as an ideal example of a Hotzenwald house now open to public view.

Entering the house by the central door along its length one comes across the corridor referred to above, the so-called "shield" which functioned as insulation both for man and beast. To the left at ground-floor level is the living area, the parlour occupying a place of distinction. In it one can recognize the most important elements making up a Black Forest living room. There is the table

*Hotzenwaldhaus.
Kitchen and econo-
mical stove with
smoke cowl above.*

with its stools and a bench as well as a tiled stove with a bench
running round it, bars for drying the washing in winter and thoroughly wet clothes after exposure to the weather outside. Near
the stove a narrow staircase leads to other rooms or the bedcham-
bers of the house. The parlour is scantily furnished, a portrait of
two of saints, a picture of Maria Theresia with whom the Hotzenwald folk were not politically affiliated. Apart from these, Joseph
Tröndle, is portrayed as an Austrian official wearing a red and
white sash. A laquered clock and glass barometer with a water fil-
ling complete the parlour inventory.

Next to the living room is the kitchen, small and dark. In it stands
an economical oven whose hearth was walled in so as to save
wood. It is overhung by a cowl of plaited branches smeared with
clay, the "Gwölm", used to catch smoke and sparks. A modest
kitchen cupboard, a table and a bench make up the entire furnis-
hings.

From the kitchen and from the parlour to the south one discovers
other rooms. In the 19th century rooms facing south were modified to provide more sleeping space. In the first a couple can be
seen in the regional costume of the 18th century. Next to the wardrobe there are documents giving an insight into the revolt of the
saltpetre workers during the 18th century. This at first was a poli-

tical movement influenced by Switzerland not far away, a movement which wanted to force both the Austrian overlords as well as those in St. Blasien to provide greater freedoms. At first this "Revolution" was led by the farmer and saltpetre worker, J. F. Albiez from Buch. In the period which followed, the objections of the saltpetre workers bore fruit in the church reforms carried out by J. H. von Wessenberg and later under the new rulers of Baden especially in the areas of schooling, tax and military service.

The central room is furnished for children or servants. The outer one to the south contains all the accessories required for weaving together with a loom of the times prior to the introduction of mechanical ones. Weaving was one of the principal occupations among the Hotzenwald inhabitants and required certain special skills, strength and endurance. For a few, weaving very quickly became a main source of income and the family name "Weaver" (Weber) confirms this fact very clearly. It is clear that weaving developed most rapidly in those areas where the soil yielded meagre crops and the practice of parcelling land which resulted in arable areas becoming smaller and smaller. This was true above all for the southern Black Forest, Hotzenwald and Wiesental. Every

Hotzenwaldhaus. Weaving room on the south side and at one time part of the "Schild".

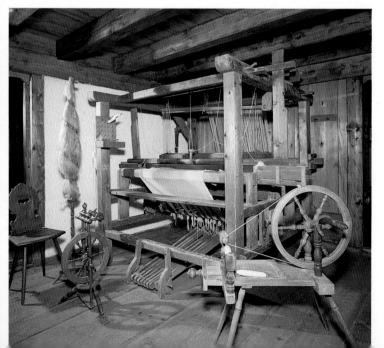

member of the family able to work was obliged to help during weaving. The children wound the yarn or wool while men and women alternated at the loom. When the warp strands were taut, the shuttle had to fly across the loom while the frame was operated by foot. It was not for nothing that folks said in those days: "Our Lord had to suffer much, but he never worked the loom." Indeed, the Hotzenwald district was so much occupied with the weaving trade that a rough cloth has been named after it – "Hotze".

On the northern side of the house, i. e. to the right of the main entrance, one comes across a stall with a feed alley. Today, this area is used for other purposes and, each year, offers the possibility to set up three or four special exhibitions dedicated to peasant or agricultural life which would otherwise be difficult to erect and document within the museum itself.

The upper storey is also the attic. It is an example of the so-called ridgepole construction where the supports are held in place as they were in the Middle Ages by driving a wooden wedge or a nail through the tenon. This was typical for threshing houses. We can see that the roof space encompasses the entrance, the threshing floor and the hayloft. The curing room and adjacent rooms also lie above the living area. The former is an upward continuation of the kitchen where meat and sausages were hung up and smoked.

The roof itself is thatched and the ends of the ridge beams are topped with bundles of straw and crosses, caps or "Chäpli" as they are called.

Just as Schauinsland follows Hotzenwald among the high-lying regions of the Black Forest on the map, so here in the Museum we move now to the "Schauinsland".

Hotzenwald-haus from the rear showing the entrance porch and "Chäppli".

13

The Schauinslandhaus ③

This is typical of the house construction found in the north-western corner of the Black Forest region occupying an area between the summits of Schauinsland, Feldberg and ranging along the high mountain valleys and cols flanked by Herzogenhorn, Hochkopf and Belchen. Here, because of the harshness of the climate and the sparse vegetation, only cattle rearing and grass cropping is possible. Despite this, the distribution of the population has been influenced by other factors such as mining and later steel and glass manufacture. These at one time were able to relieve the farmer of his products to some extent, but on the other hand gave him the opportunity to work in the mines and factories. The enormous demand for wood in this industry also led to the total denudation of the landscape during the 15th and 16th centuries. And so the area here has remained one shorn of its woods whose rolling contours offer little protection from wind and cold.

The features of the Schauinslandhaus reflect this situation. Like the Hotzenwaldhaus, it is placed parallel to the slope of the hill on which the house stands. Contrary to the latter, and indeed to all other Black Forest farmers' houses, entrance to it is at the side of the house, the door being placed in the middle. The latter is amply protected by a long, overhanging, shingled hip-roof section. A corridor round the house such as that found in the Hotzenwaldhaus is confined to the mountain side and the narrow side of the house at the back. Because at one time there was a well in this hallway it was called "Brunnenschopf". In order to offer optimal resistance to wind and weather the roof above the living area is constructed using the "lying chair" device to strengthen the supports holding up the roof. This house is constructed as one unit of

*Schauinslandhaus.
Entrance to the house on its narrow side which is protected by a shingled hip roof.*

Schauinslandhaus. View of the parlour with its table and "Herrgottswinkel" and a statue of St. Joseph.

fair size and has no outbuildings. The farmers raised the smallest cattle in Europe, the so-called "Hinterwälder Vieh" (Backwoods Cattle). In the 18th century, potatoes were cultivated on narrow strips of land. Characteristically, the farmsteads stand well away from one another on high slopes or where for a moment the land flattens a little and this is typical for the area. In the valleys they stand relatively cheek by jowl at hundred-yard intervals.

Within the Museum the Schauinsland is the youngest representative of a farmer's house. One had been keeping an eye on it since 1977 with a view to acquiring it for the Museum, but application for purchase of the "Reesehansehof" in Hofsgrund fell flat owing to an objection based on the right to residence. However, since 1982, it is possible to visit a farmhouse orientated to the Reesehanshof which is new and built to scale. It was erected with beams hewn by hand after the manner of building the original in Hofsgrund, built about 1680. One may note here that the majority of farmsteads in the Black Forest had their own names which as a rule generally outlived change of ownership. In the main, these names can be traced back to the 18th century at a time when enlightened rulers had their land surveyed and officially registered. The name then chosen generally stuck.

Schauinslandhaus. Parlour with its tiled stove and so-called "Kunstbank" (terraced seating); bars above to hang washing out to dry.

From the corridor of the house and turning right one enters the parlour which faces the valley and which is illuminated by a bay window fitted with small window panes. The "Herrgottswinkel" (Lord's Corner) is enclosed by it and shows a crucifix and a statue of St. Joseph with Child. The walls of the living-room display the usual religious pictures and family portraits. An enamelled clock and a dresser with crockery catch the eye of the visitor as well as the tiled stove with its steel bars on which to hang washing.

The kitchen next to the living-room also contains the kind of economical stove alluded to above as well as the cowl to catch smoke.

*Schauinsland-haus.
Kitchen with economical stove and smoke cowl.*

The kitchen is on two levels, the upper serving as a curing room. Next to the kitchen we come across a room fitted out as a wood-carver's workshop and documents the fact the farmers of the southern Black Forest region were very much involved in this activity as an extra source of income since the end of the 16th century, especially at the time mining came to a standstill, so forcing them to resort to this craft all the more. Wood from trees which had grown straight and which was easily split were the basic requirements for this skill which the peasants had learned from the monks at St. Blasien. They produced wooden dishes and house-

Schauinslandhaus showing wood-carver's work bench used mainly for making equipment in and around the house.

Schauinslandhaus showing wood-carver's work: three boxes used in making cheese.

hold objects such as buckets, stands, bowls, spoons, shovels, forks, wooden chests and boxes.

Proceeding through the kitchen or through a small door on the narrow side of the house brings us to the "Brunnenschopf" which, while encompassing the storage room of the house, also served as a room to work in during the cold winter months since it was protected from the weather outside. It is not surprising, therefore, to find the well here and is conveniently situated between kitchen and stall. Entrance to the "Brunnenschopf" is at the level of the house front and animals could also be directed into the stall easily. The roof on the mountain side of the house runs down as far as the supports of the "Brunnenschopf" or "well-shed" so that this and the house itself appear to be one unit.

The working area on the ground floor is made up of the feeding alley and stalls. A wall separates the sleeping quarters of the family from the stalls and this proximity certainly had two advantages. One coud hear everything that went on in the stall and in addition the bedroom gained some of the warmth from the stall. The cold, incidentally, was why the toilet was placed on the side of the house facing the valley and above the dung heap, asccessible via the bedroom along a short verandah to the exterior. Looking round the well shed and its adjacent stall we notice a number of pieces of equipment, a dummy cow and an old pig-sty. In all this it should be borne in mind that in the past both the cow and the pig were shorter, smaller and less sturdy than they are today. The upper storey of the Schauinsland house was also divided into a living area and a working area. The bedroom with its four-poster, wardrobe, chest, chair and clock was placed over the parlour. Another room was divided off by the house entrance and, above the kitchen, one finds the curing room into which kitchen smoke infiltrated through the plankwork. Thus, sides of ham, sausages and bacon were hung up and conserved. The upper part of the curing room is roofed with loosely-placed boarding which allowed the smoke to dissipate through them into the roof area. The threshing floor and the hayloft is situated opposite the living area in the upper storey and at a lower elevation. Access to it from outside is possible from the mountain side. The threshing area leads into the haystore which could be stocked from here with hay and aftergrass. Its floor was also the ceiling of the stall. The ridgepole and column construction above the working area and that above the living area is very noticeable in the Schauinslandhaus. The rigidity of the whole is further enhanced by the use of long struts. The roof itself has a hip-roof construction on all sides and is tiled with wood shingles.

On the narrow side of the house one finds a projecting, mortised board called a "Schub" (pusher). Incidentally, it is to be found on all the other houses too and its function was to keep the ceiling boards tightly together in a state of tension and thus free of grooves by repeated hammering so creating a wedge-fit.

Schauinslandhaus. Broad side of the building in which the parlour, the room, the area for livestock, the outer verandah and a toilet above the dunghill.

The Charcoal Pile ⑤

The charcoal pile is witness to charcoal-burning and for that reason has its rightful place in the Museum. It was placed here in 1972. The Baden-Württemberg Forestry Commission placed 46 m³ of beechwood at the Museum's disposal for its construction. Along with charcoal-burning on the premises of ironworks and glass-manufacturers, this activity also took place in the middle of woods or their edge within view of neighbouring houses and it is very likely that the main reason for this was the bad roads of the time making transportation difficult. Charcoal-burning on a rational and commercial scale began in the 15th century at a time when the requirements of the ironworks became noticeable.

The essence of the pile is its chimney-vent which consists of three round timbers separated from one another at a distance of about 30 centimetres and held together by iron rings. Around this arrangement there is an iron grid placed radially. Blocks and rounded pieces of wood were then placed against it in an upright position forming a kind of lower storey. On top of this comes a second layer laid in a similar way which, at the top, is covered with pieces of wood laid on the whole horizontally. Gaps were filled with extra pieces of wood. Then the whole is topped with 20 centimetres of straw and earth. Finally, the girth of the pile is encircled by planks jutting out from the pile serving as a foot board. The pile can now be ignited by tipping live charcoal down the chute followed by other pieces until the column glows, the heat then being transmitted to the surrounding wood and resulting in its carbonisation. Draught was necessary and for this purpose vents had to be made and the pile kept under constant observation.

The process of transformation where, in this incandescence, the rest of the wood was carbonised, took about eight to ten days and required a further two days to cool. As a rule, 48 waggons of wood were required to produce six waggons of charcoal per pile after burning. A medieval ironworks needed 500 waggons of charcoal annually which meant the felling of an area of some 125 hectares or 1.25 square kilometre and only wood that was at least 20 years old could be used.

The Boundary Stone of St. George's Monastery ⑥

On our way to the "Hippenseppenhof" house we pass a boundary stone which displays a cross and an abbot's crosier belonging to the monastery of St George which played an important part in the history of this region. It was founded in the 11th century, removed to Villingen in 1633 after having been destroyed and was finally dissolved in 1806.

Charcoal pile - testimony of a trade carried on well away from the farmer's house and yard. The roofing you see here is simply for protective purposes.

Boundary stone belonging to St. Georgen Monastery in the Black Forest and witness to former system of "patchwork" states.

21

The "Hippenseppenhof" ⑦

The third farmhouse on our tour through the Museum is an example of what the people of the Black Forest call a "Heidenhaus" (lit. heathen house). From the point of view of its construction it represents the oldest type of house and is also that most frequently encountered. It can be described as a large house. The type belongs to the central highlands of the Black Forest where the climate is damp and in a region providing woodland and pasture as well as arable land. For this reason, farming is carried on in practically enclosed economic units and this is the predominant feature here. The essential countryside to which the **Heidenhaus** belongs with its high, wild valleys and lonely grazing slopes was a later colonised area in the Black Forest, lying between Kinzigtal in the north and the Dreisam, Höllen and Wutach Valleys in the south. The most important characteristics of the **Heidenhaus** are as follows: The house stands vertical to the mountain slope so that the farmer can drive his waggon straight into the attic. A massive, overhanging hip roof runs down the front side of the house. The ground floor encompasses both the living area and that housing livestock, the former comprising parlour and kitchen. The consequence of the ridgepole and column construction precludes total enclosure of the attic and so the door is not positioned in the centre of the hip towards the hill. This kind of timbering began to decline by about 1600 and was subsequently displaced by the so-called "lying chair" construction which then became dominant. As though to underline its age and the difference in construction, the new form was referred to as "heathen" i. e. the Black Forest **Heidenhaus.**

The **Hippenseppenhof** to be seen in the Museum was erected in the year 1599 in Katzensteig near Furtwangen, an area within the sphere of influence of the monastery at St. Blasien. During 1965/66, the farm at Katzensteig was dismantled and re-erected here. Its name derives from the fact that its owner, one Joseph Fehrenbach, originally hailed from a locality called "Hippen", actually a strip of land near Escheck, Furtwangen, some 200 years ago. The roof-ridge turret with its bell may well only go back to the 18th or 19th century.

The "Hippenseppenhof" belongs to the older form of the **Heidenhaus** which houses livestock on the valley side. It is divided by a broad feed alley. On each side the cows of the **Hinterwald** stock stood in their byres. The floor planking is removeable. Grass and straw clippings lay underneath and when this was thoroughly impregnated with urine it was spread on the fields as dung or sent to

Hippenseppenhof. Columns supporting the roof are of very substantial construction. View from the stall to the living quarters. The roof with its silvery shingles covering an area of approx. 2100 sq.ft. (700 qm).

saltpetre workers who extracted that substance from it. In their turn, they sold the saltpetre to gunpowder manufacturers or metal processors. Cowbells can be seen hanging on the wall. One of these was worn by the leading cow on the long trek to the old city cattle markets. Since the destination was often Paris, the bell bears the inscription "A Paris". The band is richly decorated with smaller bells. The straw plaiting on the valley side wall presents a problem until we are told that it was a cape for the young cowherds as a protection against rain. It appears odd to us today. Passing to the outside from the stall, we notice the well-trough, the milk depository and a whetstone. Past the whetstone along the house wall we enter the living area of the house by a divided door.

23

Hippenseppenhof showing the parlour with its table and "Herrgottswinkel". The richly-decorated wall and the spoon line are easily recognizable.

Inside, one way leads to the kitchen and parlour at ground level, while another leads to the upper storeys. The "Deuchelbohrer" which hang on the wall are impressive. They were used to bore out pine-tree trunks along their length so that they could be used as water conduits. The juicer was used to make juice or wine, especially the much-beloved bilberry wine. The pearl wreaths to be seen above the chest at the end of the corridor were used on All Saints Day, and in the case of death, to lay on the grave. Again, in the parlour the richly-decorated "Herrgottswinkel" (The Lord's Corner or Alcove) can be observed. There is a statue to the Virgin Mary and colourful depictions of the saints in back-glass pictures typical of the Black Forest (Hinterglasmalerei). And if this sacred domestic alcove is distinguished by the so-called "Herrgottssäule" (God's pillar), then the other two corner supports were not any the less decorated with religious objects and icons. One notes the crucifix and rosary and the cross used for the last sacraments in the family. The "Herrgottswinkel" also contains the table and the spoon-line on which spoons hung used at table and which were replaced – without too much washing – on the line.

Opposite the "Herrgottswinkel" and table stands a large tiled stove with an adjoining oven, the "Kunst" equipped with a bench. The adjacent oven also received heat from that in the kitchen. This had the advantage that the stove seat was always warm, not only in winter, but also in spring and autumn. The larger stove was also heated from the kitchen hearth. Both chimneys to the two ovens led off to the kitchen. Above the "Kunst" is a niche in which food could be kept warm. To the left of the larger stove there is a hatch to the kitchen, an old device and sensible, because one could not eat in the kitchen on account of the smoke. On the mountain side of the parlour the "Stegenkasten" can still be seen which led from the parlour into the farming couple's sleeping quarters upstairs. Warm air could be led off up into the bedroom during the evening.

There are also watches, family pictures and pictures of military service decorating the walls. In front of the stove stands the spinning wheel with its distaff and reel.

While the parlour is only at one level, the kitchen, as in the other houses, is at two levels. Above the kitchen range we find the huge cowl to catch sparks and smoke plaited of twigs and smeared with loam. After the smoke has risen through a hole in the roof it then

Hippenseppenhof. Directly opposite the table we find the tiled stove with decorated wall, a distaff, reel and spinning wheel.

Hippenseppenhof showing its kitchen with an old table-stove, open hearth and huge smoke cowl.

disperses in the attic. In this way, the sides of bacon and other meats including sausage were fumigated or cured. Near the bellows one can see the smoke vents from the range and parlour stove. Cooking utensils are minimal, and the fact that this large kitchen was used for other purposes, especially in winter, can be confirmed by the presence of other objects such as a carving bench as well as a chopping block and a kind of grid on which to slaughter animals and dismember them. In addition, there is a butter vat

Hippenseppenhof. Kitchen with butter vat for pounding and a relatively modern butter-making machine dating back to about 1900 which is frequently and amusingly confused with a washing machine.

and a buttermaking machine of later date and one or two butter models. The last objects alluded to testify to the extensive production of milk products and animals for slaughter in the Black Forest region. The upper storey of this house consists of the upper corridor, the farmer's bedroom, several rooms to accommodate servants and children and the hayloft. Various objects used in straw plaiting are noticeable in the corridor, an activity which is known to have been carried out since the 18th century in the Triburg area. At the far end there is a glass case containing regional headwear which exhibits a remarkable collection of the well-

Hippenseppenhof. The bedroom furniture is colourfully decorated with monograms of Christ and the Virgin Mary.

known "bulb hats" and which points up both the variety and the development of regional costume accessories. Among them, one can also see the oldest examples of the bulb hat.

Going upstairs, we come across the bedchamber with its four-poster, chest and wardrobe, cradle,clock and chamber pot. It is of colourful aspect and decorated with religious symbols which signify the farmer's devotional aspirations. The bed itself had practical advantages; it protected the incumbent from the cold, draughts and gout. Its shortness may account for the fact that people were generally smaller at one time and that they slept more

27

Hippenseppenhof. Log carts standing on the ramp.

Hippenseppenhof. The buggy and its wickerwork construction.

or less in a sitting position supported by a mountain of cushions at their backs.

Opposite this bedroom were servants' rooms which are used as display rooms today.

In the attic the visitor will notice the roof construction and a whole variety of farming equipment, carts and coaches as well as an

Hippenseppenhof. Sketch graphically shows the construction of the roof supports.

old device for chopping up feed or for grinding meal. Looking up and along the roof timbers he will find the skull of an ox perched at the top of the first roof truss. After having carted all the wood for construction of the house, the ox would then be slaughtered the day the roofing timbers were in place and its skull displayed to ward off plagues, lightning and accident. At this point we find ourselves amid a diversity of signs and symbols, religious, magical and superstitious, carved into the walls of the threshing room. There are pre-Christian symbols for fertility, healing, the blessing of children and the harvest. One can recognize the six-pointed star, the sunwheel, the tree of life, a heart, the leaning cross and the heraldic lozenge. Among the Christian symbols there are churches, a heart with three swords, the letters C-M-B and the ABC. The last recalls the custom of dedicating the alphabet to God so that He may formulate an appropriate prayer. Of interest,

Hippenseppenhof. The walls of the threshing floor showing abundance of carved symbols. Churches are recognizable as well as the tail of the much-feared Halley comet.

Hippenseppenhof The cross of St. Longinus protects the stall side of the building.

too, is Halley's Comet over a church auguring catastrophe for human kind. It seems that symbols for fending off evil played a large role in the beliefs of Black Forest inhabitants. Lines ending in points with varying numbers, the pentagramme, the devil's or witches knot and the ox-skull already alluded to. The farmer's personal sign can also be assumed since it appears as the sign of ownership of the house, on felled wood and on farming implements. The **Hippenseppenhof** roof has a total area of some 2100 sq, ft, and is tiled with 70,000 shingles whose form one can quite easily notice at the entry to the granary. Here, too, one can see the pulley whereby dung and washed-away soil could be hoisted and then spread on the steep fields.

The great cross of Longinus on the front of the stalls is there to protect and ward off danger, but also as a warning. This special depictive form of a crucifixion with its implements of torture and St. Longinus is widespread in the vicinity of the Rophrarsberg near Triberg, near Furtwangen, in Schönwald and in the Prech and Elz Valleys. According to the so-called Pilate documents, the soldier who pierced Christ's side was called Longinus. Later, this same man was martyred as bishop in Cappadocia. His feast day falls on the 15th March.

The Black Forest Barn ⑧

The **Heidenhaus** farmsteads possessed ancillary buildings and among these the Museum exhibits a granary and a private chapel.

The **Hippenseppenhof** granary shown here was built in 1590 on the property of the Winterhaldershof in Schollach, and transferred in 1969. It served as a granary, as a food store and as a place of safe-keeping for documents. As a rule, the grain store did not stand downwind of the farmhouse and was erected on posts as a protection against damp. The door and the steps leading to it are protected by an overhanging roof. The doors to the granary give on to a central passage along the axis of the building and on both sides of this there are boxes in which the grain is stored according to kind and quality. Bread baked every four weeks was put away together with the smoked meats. On boards at the side, material for making clothes was stored. Also worth noticing are the nets and other apparatus for catching fish. At the very end of the granary there is a secret chamber entered by a door cunningly set

The Black Forest granary shows fruit boxes on left and right as well as fishing tackle and food-storage containers.

in the wall. This was the farm archive and in it were the farmer's most important legal documents together with money kept locked up in his private chest.

It was rare to see a chapel as part of the building complex. It served as a place for personal prayer and devotion.

The Farm's Private Chapel ⑨

The **Hippenseppenhof** private chapel (1736) was once part of the Simonshof in Jostal before re-erection at the Museum in 1967. A chapel of this kind belongs to the larger, outlying farms and was seldom used to celebrate mass, being in the main a place for devotions and the daily prayers of the family and servants. Its bell rang for prayer, but almost certainly as a summons to table as well. The depiction above the altar protrays St. John the Baptist, Simon, Andrew and St. Anthony the Hermit. It is quite likely that St. Simon was placed in the foreground because the donor of the altar was named Simon Fehrenbacher according to the inscription. Additionally, this saint was also patron of woods and woodsmen as is to be seen from his saw. St John and St Anthony were revered as patrons of livestock and farmers as their attributes (lamb, pig and ox) show. St. Andrew for his part had special significance in the matter of love, marriage and fertility and so the entire estate and its activities were in good hands. The saints were a guarantee for the well-being of the farm. However, one might ask what function the roe's skull had in front of the altar and which was found on removing the chapel. Does it say anything about the reason for building a chapel or does it say something in general about the chapel being a fitting place for a saint since the roe is traditionally associated with just this, and always leads to the saint in legend? The roe is said to protect and to nourish the saint and symbolises as well the need to return to Christ. Seen thus, the skull could signify safety under God's patronage to whom one prayed at this private shrine. Looking round, we also notice a statue of St. Catherine, pictures painted on glass and two votive pictures. These were placed there by the faithful for varying reasons, but mostly as thankful acknowledgement for help received.

The chapel at Hippenseppenhof is richly decorated inside. You will see the wooden altar, votive pictures, a statue of St. Catherine and paintings on glass.

The "Vogtsbauernhof" ⑩

Passing the garden belonging to **Hippenseppenhof** which is marked off by an ancient crucifix and then by several small fields planted with the most important crops grown in the Black Forest, the visitor approaches the imposing form of the **Vogtsbauernhof** which, according to a particular type of house to be found in this area is called the Gutach house after the place of that name. It is to be found in that region administrated by the former authorities of Hornberg and St. Georgen which also includes Gutach and the neighbouring region to the east. The richly varied nature of the landscape together with a mild climate allows pasture land and cattle-breeding combined with forestry. The broad valleys also make it possible for fruit to be grown.

The most important feature of the Gutach house can be seen from afar, the light-coloured stone walling in the centre of its house frontage facing the valley. Behind these stones and timbering lies the kitchen which is adjacent to the parlour and another room.

The roof construction of the house is that of the so-called "leaning chair" type (liegender Dachstuhl). The narrower sides of the house are protected by an overhanging hip roof enclosing verandahs and house entrances. The height of the guttering and ridge as well as the breadth in relation to its overall height together produce a well-proportioned farmer's house. Its Renaissance decoration shows evidence of Strasbourg's influence in the Kinzig Valley and upwards. It is probable, too, that it was from here that the decisive influences came which affected the course of the Reformation. The Gutach house type was in all likelihood brought into being on the 1st March, 1568 in Stuttgart where a new building regulation was laid down. This stipulated that in future the kitchen, because of its susceptibility to fire, be surrounded by either stone walling or a timbered frame. Building tradition in the Black Forest which at that time was only familiar with wooden walls of posts and planks now saw itself forced to place a protected kitchen of this sort in the middle of the house, that is, between the parlour and another room, and whenever one comes across this fact it can be immediately recognized as a house belonging to the Württemberg sphere of influence. In addition to this, one can also see that the layout of the interior, too is in conformity with Protestant taste and mentality.

The **Vogtsbauernhof** did not have to be re-erected in this place, but has always stood here. Indeed, we know that the farm prior to it goes back to 1425 when it was sold to a certain Franz Bernbach

Vogtsbauernhof, built on this spot about 1570, formed the nucleus of the Gutach Museum opened to the public in 1964.

Vogtsbauernhof.
The Bible to be seen in the
corner column is evidence of
protestant piety.

by Rainold von Urslingen and his spouse, Anastasia von Üsen-
berg, the latter having previously been married to Werner von
Homburg and from whom she inherited the so-called "Wählerhof" in Gutach. In their turn, the inheritors to Bernbach left these
farms and lands to the **Heiligenpflegern** of the parish church at
Hornberg on the 21st January, 1447. In 1491, the proceeds from
these farms served to provide a living for the chaplain of Hornberg's church who read mass there. Later, in 1536, this ecclesia-
stical property was accommodated during the Reformation by
Württemberg's rulers, secularised, and appropriated as a means
of support for Hornberg's poor. Both the **Wählerhof** and **Vogtsbauernhof** remained property under stewardship serving the poor
of the parish. They were frequently in the hands of one family for
long periods. The latter, for example, up to the Thirty Years War
belonged to a family called Tescher and Moser and thereafter up
until the end of the 18th century to one Wälde or Weldin, later
the name Aberle appears as far as the 19th century when ownership had to be shared by a third party. This situation lasted until
1963 right up until the time the Wolfach regional council purcha-
sed the property from three inheritors to establish farm and lands
as the nucleus of an open-air museum for the Black Forest. Bar-
bara Aberle, the last owner-farmer, left at the end of 1965.

Just why the farm carried the name "Vogtsbauernhof" is not as
clear as it might be, despite the well-known story. The word
"Vogt" can mean "prefect", "magistrate", "warden" or "over-
seer". One thing is certain, the "Vogtsbauer" (farmer-overseer)
was the richest among the farmers of the **Wählerhof** and as such
perhaps also invested with certain authority as an officer of the
law and executive for Hornberg. Old deeds relating to the farm
reveal that after 1570 the **Vogtsbauernhof** was erected having

stalls and barn under one roof. Entering the front door whose left post has the farm's house symbol carved into it, the visitor finds himself in the hallway which extends across the entire first floor. Adjacent to it along its length are, to the valley side, the parlour, kitchen and back rooms ranging toward the mountain side as well as the access to the stalls. The parlour lying to the front was the focal point of the household. Here, meals were taken; here one spent the evening or continued to work during it. Here, too, the farmer conducted his business as bailiff. In the "Herrgottswinkel" the family Bible is lodged in a niche of the corner column, a custom among pious Württemberg protestants. Portraits of the saints are

Vogtsbauernhof. View of the other table in the parlour and the tiled stove. It's probable that the farmer held the office of bailiff and supervised the five other farms in the district.

therefore missing, and only representations of the Last Supper and the Burial of Christ were allowed. Diametrically opposite the table and the Bible corner one finds the huge tiled stove with its "terraced" seats. Here was the familial central point of the parlour. The visitor will recognize various developments in lighting in

37

Vogtsbauernhof. The kitchen smoke cowl extends to the length of the kitchen. Two stoves suggest that there were two parties in the house in the 19th century.

the pinewood-chip light on its stone slab, the simple oil lamp above the round table and petroleum lamp at the window. This room, too, has a stairway leading off to the bedrooms above it. The chimney flue arches over the entire width of the kitchen and within it meats and sausages were smoked above the economical stove of which two can be seen today. the base of a third is recognisable on the floor, and is evidence of the fact that the house was used by three parties in the 19th and 20th centuries. The smoke left the oven either directly to the outside or escaped through a chimney of planks on the gable side leading up to the house-ridge and so to the open air.

The room to the back on the ground floor was used mainly by the farmer in retirement and today serves for museum purposes and is inaccessible to the visitor. At the far end of the corridor there are two rooms used in the 19th century as living rooms, but before that they were used for other purposes. At the rear of both one finds old photos and models of different types of houses to be found in the Black Forest. The stalls are immediately adjacent to the rooms and this area, too, is divided by a feed alley, the animals standing perpendicularly to it. The cowbells with their bands are unique to Gutach and are worth looking at. The stall ends in a walled cellar for crop storage. Sheep could be kept in a pen under the ramp leading to the attic.

The **Vogtsbauernhof** upper storey is divided into a number of rooms used for different purposes. The first of these is the main bedroom with its four-poster, two cupboards, chest, two cradles and two stools. The furniture is in part ornamentally painted and partly without ornament, flat and sober. The contrast to **Hippenseppenhof** is striking. In the room at the rear slept the old farmer and his wife as "dependants". So here, too, we find a four-poster

Vogtsbauernhof. The bedroom furniture is subdued in colour.

Vogtsbauernhof. The 17th cent. loom puts one in mind of the self-sufficiency of farmer who also had to work with basic material to make this own clothing.

again, a cupboard and two chests. In the house corridor hang the tools used for work in the woods. In the deeds of the Gutach farms there are various sorts of linen cloth mentioned made from flax and hemp fibre on home looms and so it is that the lower room opposite the parlour is fitted out with a large loom. It stems from the 17th century and comes from Prechtal nearby and is a gift from the city of Lahr.

As a rule, the farmer working on the remote farms of the Black Forest was obliged to do most jobs himself. Skilled farmers would specialise in certain crafts, and later put this to advantage by going to work for a small firm as farmers on a daily wage basis. The interior appointments of a farm especially the supply of clothes, shoes and apparatus to farms was essentially the work of the craftsman. In plying their trade they were then the farmer's guest, ate, lived and stayed the night there according to what had to be done. Because they were always on the move, they managed to evade the strict control of the guilds and thereby upset their regulations. Such "farmers" were therefore referred to as "on the applecart" or as "going on the applecart". As we said, they were often put up by the farmer that led to many a tale which has come

down to us via the pen of H. Hansjakob. Apropos of all this there is a saying which is still in circulation: "Hey, Mum, put another ladleful of water to the soup; the tailor's coming." Finally, these "applecart men" were welcome visitors to all the members of a family living far from the mainstream of events, and who, after all, led pretty lonely lives because of their remotenes. Quite often these gentlemen proved themselves well-informed and highly-skilled matchmakers.

Of considerable importance to farms cultivating fruit and other crops was the work of the basket-maker and his products made of wickerwork. His working area catches the eye in one of the rooms of this storey.

It is also clear that the farmer's and his servants required good shoes, and for this reason the shoemaker was often at the farm for several days at a time before he had satisfied everyone's needs. And so it is that his work, too, is recorded here at the museum. Looking around this workroom we discover an old lathe which testifies to the work of the carpenter. He was responsible for the variety of furniture needed for bedroom, parlour and kitchen.

If the tradesman lived from his daily wage and the proceeds of his own small farm run by the members of his family, then both farm-

Vogtsbauernhof. An original farmhand's room re-arranged as a bedroom for a retired farming couple.

hands and maids had to rely only on the work of their hands. They undertook this kind of work either because they hailed from very poor homes or were simply obliged to do such work because they were not eligible to an inheritance within the family, and therefore not able to set up on their own as farmers. These servants who, frequently enough, were concerned with the problems and education of the farmer's children, were housed in narrow, unheated rooms in which, as a rule, there was a bed and a chest, a chamber pot and perhaps a picture. It was often the case that these rooms

42

Vogtsbauernhof. Sketch graphically portraying the so-called "lying chair" roofing timbers.

were later transformed into accommodation for the aged farmer and his wife in which case some kind of heating had to be installed.

Since the **Vogtsbauernhof** was built after 1570 it displays the most modern form of roofing, the so-called "lying chair" construction. In such a construction the roof itself "sits" on supports which look like a leaning chair. The attic itself can be driven into over a ramp situated in the central section of the house. The entrance gives on to the threshing floor and from thence into a large workroom. Normally, there is plenty of space for farming equipment in the attic and this usually contained a plough, one or two harrows, a waggon that could be adapted for a number of jobs, a cart, chains and a sledge which one could use in the woods as well as over the fields., However, a museum is concerned to collect

Vogtsbauernhof. Attic showing many farming implements collected by the Museum.

and display as many pieces of equipment as possible that are steadily becoming rarer, and thus one finds many pieces of apparatus used on the fields here, but also those used in bringing in the harvest as well as a mill for separating chaff from grain and also its forerunners. These are the grain vats in which the corn and chaff was shaken until the latter rose to the top and could easily be removed. But, of course, before this could take place the harvest had to be brought in. In this the most important implements were the sickle, the scythe, hayfork and rake. All these were partly or wholly of wood up to 1900 and were made on the farm. Before use, the scythe blade was hardened by hammering and sharpened on the whetstone. For centuries only the sickle was used to harvest the corn whereby the stalks were cut rather high. The ears were then bundled and thereafter laid up in the attic for the time

Vogtsbauernhof. Attic showing the historical development of the plough from the simplest "claw" plough to the adjustable plough.

being until time allowed for cheir threshing in the autumn and winter. This was undertaken by four men on the threshing floor who swung their flails onto the sheaves laid out before them until the grain and chaff were separated. Both were then swept up and subsequently placed in the grain vat or separator. The development of the plough in this region may well be of particular interest to visitors who can watch its modifications here as if on a historical stage. The oldest tool is the single-shoe plough which in the main consisted of three elements viz, the plough beam to which the drawing animal was attached, the handle and a curved piece of wood acting as a share. Later, at the end of the 19th century, another form takes its place which enables the plough to be turned more easily and, at the end of the furrow, the shares could be swung round.

Vogtsbauernhof. Outstanding example of a so-called Gutach House at the Museum one of the most-photographed houses in the Black Forest.

46

47

The Gutach Granary ⑪

On leaving the **Vogtsbauernhof** via the ramp entrance we see an apple crusher to our right. A vertical millstone mashed the apples into a wooden trough which were then further pressed by a fruit crusher or winepress.

A farmhouse in the central Black Forest area generally had several neighbouring buildings which on the one hand served the interests of security or fulfilled a special function. Thus, the granary

The Gutach granary with its stone base and wooden upper storey housed various fruits for safe-keeping, provision and raw material for clothing and guaranteed continued existence when catastrophe struck.

Gutach granary.
The horn of plenty as symbol
of its function.

Gutach granary.
Representation of a ploughshare, the
commonest symbol of farming life.

was always somewhat removed from the main building where, in
the case of fire, at least grain for bread, meat reserves and important house documents would be preserved. The granary on show
here dates back to the first thirty years of the 17th century, was
built in Oberharmersbach and re-erected here in 1963 as a museum piece. It consists of a stone lower storey into whose facing
stones a ploughshare and a horn of plenty have been chiselled.
The wooden storage area itself is surrounded by an arbour-like
walk, the "Trippel". The farmer stored barrelled must and wine
in the lower storey as well as bread, apples, garden and field produce intended to keep over winter. The wooden part of the building housed privisions, spirits, basic clothing material, hemp,
wool and animal skins as well as three harvests of threshed corn.
In this way the continued existence of the farm was assured in the
case of conflagration, bad harvest and hailstorm. One could even
hold out for a whole year with a three harvest stock and on top of
this the seeds for a further year assured the family of survival.
Salt, so important for human life, was preserved in a small sack
tucked away in a secret, built-in locker. The peculiarity of this
granary is its two-roomed construction. The smaller half served as
a storeroom for the retired members of the family.

The bakehouse and distillery ⑬

In the interests of safety, the bakehouse and distillery also stood some way from the farmhouse. That to be seen here originally belonged to the **Vogtsbauernhof** complex and was erected in 1870. The oven has room for 14 standard loaves. Cake as well as apples, pears, damsons, slices of beet and cabbage leaves were also baked in it. In addition, it was also used for retting hemp and flax.

The oven is oval-shaped above which arches the so-called "vault" made from firebrick. Its foundation is of the same material embedded in a layer of sand. The smokestack rises at one end of the vault and is led back over it towards the front so that the hot gases can give off heat to the oven itself. The oven is fed through what is called its "mouth" firstly with wood to heat it and then with the kneaded loaves after the ash has been brushed away.

In the still itself a mash of fruit was heated giving rise to a vapour containing alcohol which was then cooled by passing it through cold water. The spirits flowed into the receiving vessel.

View of the bakehouse and distillery belonging to Vogtsbauernhaus erected around 1870. The "mouth" of the oven and the distilling apparatus can be seen.

The "knock" or "thud" saw, an important monument to technical development in the Black Forest from the 13th century to 1800.

The sawmill ⑭

The long-roofed building housing the sawmill was built in 1673 on the Willmershof in Schwärzenbach and re-erected on museum land in 1963. The operation of the saw belongs to one of the oldest forms of sawmill in the Black Forest. The mechanism has been used since 1245 and only around 1800 was it replaced by the upward-stroke saw.

Water sets the millwheel in motion, this in turn motivates the axletree on which there are three lugs called heavers. As the axle revolves, these lift the saw-frame which, as it descends, saws through the stem of the tree. The up and down motion of the saw-frame can be re-inforced or slowed up by pliable pine rods on which the frame hangs. These in their turn are tensed under the roof of the mill. The falling of the frame caused a thudding which could be heard a long way off and so the saw is referred to as a "thud saw".

The apiary with its plaited baskets and sandstone walls recalls the fact that Black Forest honey was the only way to sweeten dishes up to about 1800.

The apiary ⑮

The beehive or free-standing apiary is to be found in the orchard. Its sandstone walls come from a hive that until 1968 stood in Prechtal. These walls could still be saved in time during building operations. They are a gift from the Baden Beekeepers' Association by arrangement with the Beekeepers' Club in Oberelztal. The original apiary could well date back to about 1875 and has been constructed using stones from the "Heidburg". In 1968, what was left of it came into the care of the Museum. It stands here in recognition of the fact that up to about 1800 the only way to sweeten dishes was to use Black Forest honey. The oldest factories to manufacture honey from sugar beet date from about this period. In the old days the bees lived in baskets of plaited straw rope placed in shelves which were smooth and even. In the lowest ring of straw there is a hole cut into it to allow the bees access. Sometimes the board or shelf had a five centimeter-long channel cut into it as a ramp for the bees. If, during the summer, the swarm was large then the beekeeper would place a somewhat smaller "house" of the same construction under the original where the bees would build new combs and where further honey could be deposited. The bees would withdraw into the original hive over the winter and the "house" would be taken away. Harvesting the honey usually took place in February when the hive would be cut from the board. In so doing the hive would be turned upside down. The bees would then be driven into one half of the hive by smoke and while thus in retreat the lower half would be cleared of its honey with a sharp knife. The next year would see the other half thus cut out, in other words, always the older half. After salvaging the honey, the hive would be replaced on the shelf. From March onwards the queen would then begin to lay and the rest of the community be busy tending the young and building new combs in the empty part of the hive. The extracted combs would be covered and then taken to the honey vat and left to drip. The honey separator has only been known since the end of the 19th century.

*Entrance to
a beehive.*

The mill and the rammer (16)

Probably there is no other building which seems to us more native to the Black Forest than the mill. Propagated by popular song and supported by unforgettable melodies, the Schwarzwald mill is known to all. The mills we see in the Museum were originally erected in 1609 on the Adamshof in Vorderlehensgericht. The millwork and the barley stamper were re-erected here in 1964. The right to run a mill or to establish one at all ws at one time a royal one. Later, princes and overlords on widening their spheres of influence attributed that right unto themselves. This can be confirmed by the many letters of request to the Duke of Württemberg asking for permission to erect a mill. Somewhere at the end of the 18th century and especially in the 19th century, such petitions fell into decay. The miller had now become a specialist in his own right and a craftsman, obliged to live from his own exertions. The time had come where every mill was assigned to a specific district which could encompass several villages. This resulted in the fact that many farmer's mills in individual valleys and outlying areas gradually fell into disuse.

Milling in the Black Forest probably goes back to the 13th century. They were founded on the discovery that water power with the help of a mill wheel and an axletree in a vertical position could be tranformed by simple gearwork into a horizontal motion activating the millstone. The box in which the flour is separated from the husks first came into being in the 16th century. This marked the technical completion of the mill.

The visitor to the Museum can experience for himself with the help of a guide how water sets a somewhat smaller and narrower

Corn grinder at Vogtsbauernhof.

View of the interior of the corn grinder showing funnel, mill, camshaft and bran box.

Corn husks were blown through this "Kleiekotzer" from the bran box into the husk trough.

water wheel in motion. This is connected inside the mill to an axle which rotates with it. A cog is attached to the rotating axle which engages with the mule-frame carriage or piston. This runs horizontally and activates the runner stone via the stone spindle. The runner stone traverses the stationary grinding stone and so grinds the corn which has been funnelled to them from above. From here the ground material passes to a pouch box equipped with a shaker connected with the mule-frame carriage and thus bran is separated from husk, the latter remaining in the box. The husks, however, flow through the so-called "Kleikotzer" (husk-belcher!) which is in the form of a carved human face and into the husk trough. According to legend the "Kleiekotzer" is there to discourage all wicked spirits and evil forces from entering the mill at this point and thereby preserve the bran from harm. Kinzigtal farms, too, used to have these or similar masks in the 17th century. Reports and sayings that have come down to us speak of spirit called the "Schrättele" which produced an attack of suffocation, the masks being there as protection. It is a strange fact these heads as well as the **Kleiekotzer** wear an expression that is homely and endearing, rather than one of demonic aspect which might ward off evil. Access to the mill itself consists of a double door, the upper half allowing dust to escape to the outside while the lower prevented pigs and enterprising fowl from entering. The mill's roofing is

Corn pounders in the mill. They ground material for mash and for soups.

of two kinds, the older thatching where straw was loosely laid and the later form where the straw was bundled and combed before laying. Inside the mill we can also find a rammer or stamper which at one time used to pound barley to groats, but was also used to stamp millet, spelt, hayflowers and occasionally hemp. The pounder itself consists of an oak block of wood with two hollowed-out depressions in it. Directly above them are two beechwood rammers which are raised by lugs both attached to them and the mill axle. They fall freely and so crush the material in the hollow.

The Württemberg boundary stone ⑰

Between **Vogtsbauernhof** and **Lorenzenhof,** we come across a boundary stone bearing the coat of arms of the House of Württemberg with its three antlers and that of the catholic Fürstenberg bearing a crown and eagle. The stone is placed so as to indicate which farm belongs to which administration.

*Bird's eye view of the whole museum in Gutach.
(By kind permission of the Reg. Präsidium in Karlsruhe).* ►

Boundary stone between Württemberg and Fürstenberg showing the three stag antlers of the principality of Württemberg.

The Kinzig Valley granary ⑱

This granary comes from Reutehof in the neighbouring district of Einbach-Hauserbach. The wooden section was erected in 1601. When the stone base of the building was added in 1746, the upper, wooden storey was taken over as well because of the scarcity of wood at the time. The whole was transferred here as one unit in 1972.

This granary is a smaller edition so to speak of the so-called Kinzig Valley house as one can see by comparing it here with the **Lorenzenhof.** All the elements characteristing the form of this house are also reflected in the design of the granary. Thus, it possesses a stone first storey on which the wooden granary itself is mounted. It is built on a columnar principle, oak pillars supporting and holding together a rectangular framework. There are two chambers in this granary, one of which is often popularly referred to as the "bride's chamber" because it was used by the farmer's nubile daughter. And so it was that the granary became the place where "opportunity is offered for nocturnal cohabitation and where other clandestine appointments are tacitly countenanced." This, at least, is how it was austerely expressed in 1757 on the issue of an

This Kinzigtal granary is a miniature of the Kinzigtal house with its stone base and wooden granary part.

The Kinzigtal granary with its stock of wine and cider, fruit stored for winter, washing equipment and other tackle.

order from the Fürstenberg princes condemning the practice. Apparently, it was a means of initiating marriage and subject to a strict, unwritten law whereby the problem of who should inherit the farm also played an inherent role. That this was the case is borne out by both the official reference above and by popular allusion.

The cellar housed both cider and wine barrelled in various kegs of wood. Trestles, funnels and other equipment having to do with winemaking are to be found here as well as the so-called leaching-set. This was concerned with washing clothes where a lye was used consisting of beechwood ash wrapped in a piece of cloth and boiled with the dirty linen. The word "Aschentusch" (ash-cloth

Kinzig Valley granary. Leaved cornering, the sign of a good carpenter.

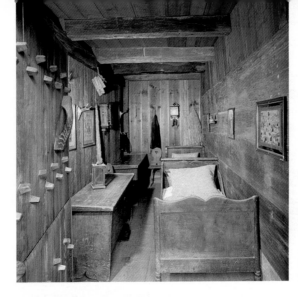

Kinzigtal granary. Servants' bedroom with meagre furnishing.

or bag) crops up again and again in old household inventories. The leaching-set consisted of a large tub, a wooden spoon and other vessels for water.

Provisions were stored and often wrapped up for the winter in the cellar. The wooden upper storey of the granary has a narrow room next to which are provisions for storing fruit according to kind in various compartments. Behind, there is a spacious room and in front of this and behind the smaller room there is a space, and then the door to the outside. The small room and the fruit compartments are only accessible from the surrounding walk running along the front side of the house and along its length. The small room is dark since there is only a little light entering through a small hatch in the outer wall. This is where the young farmhand slept or the lad that watched the farmer's sheep. The fittings are correspondingly bare. The larger room, on the other hand, was for the daughter of the house or also for maidservants. The walls of these chambers and the rest of the granary building were of vertical boards, the planks of the fruit store, however, are very carefully fitted together. Between the ceiling and the fruit store and under the roof there is an intermediate space where farming equipment was stowed. To the rear of the building on the left there is a stair up to the attic which projects over the front of the building, while the attic's interior consists of the "lying chair" construction and ridge supports. To the front, the roof is constructed as a half hip after the Kinzig Valley tradition; to the rear, the roof is lengthened and closed by a full hip. This provides roofing for parked carts, especially for the "Bennewägele" or straw-

Kinzig Valley granary. Fruit boxes containing various grains and cereals as well as a variety of apparatus.

topped buggy used to take the farmer to church or to the next town.

In front of the granary there is a shrine placed there as a warning to repentence and recalling a murder. In 1835, a jealous young farmhand shot his rival who was having an affair with one of the farmer's maids. The inscription reads: "At this place of sorrow, Michael Matt, aged 26, employed as a farmhand by Philipp Harter, was shot down in all innocence while going home on the 25th October, 1835, between six and seven in the evening. In mourning, his parents, Joseph Matt." The lady in question was probably Franziska Keller whose name appears on the side of the stone.

Shrine erected in 1835 recalling the murder of a young farmhand.

Lorenzenhof ㉠

The mightly gable of the **Lorenzenhof** farm seals off the northern end of the Museum's premises in the direction of the Gutach Valley. This house embodies the characteristics of the Kinzig Valley type of house found in the Black Forest and also widely distributed in the Acher and Rench valleys. Since these regions enjoyed a more moderate climate, it was also favourable for crop-growing and for fruit cultivation. Unlike the other houses in the Museum, this one possesses a stone cellar which also has an area for a stable. On this foundation there is a wooden upper storey having two rooms one of which is the parlour. The one corner and its room has a gangway round it. A huge thatched, hip-roof protects the house on the valley side. Both the living area and the stable are referred to here as "the house", and also attached to the house on the slope side is the barn which reaches from ground level to beneath the the roof. The fact that this construction must have penetrated into the valleys of the central Black Forest area is to be seen from the so-called "nut-stage" or "smoke-shelf" which in fact is a modified half storey found in the houses in the Hanau region not far from Strasbourg. This **Lorenzenhof** was re-erected here in 1971/72.

It had been recognized as one of the loveliest of the Kinzig Valley farmhouses still preserved in 1970, but application for purchase, its dismantling in Oberwolfach and re-erection on Museum land took a long time. Built in 1540 and stemming from the principality of Fürstenberg, it is the oldest house in the Museum. It is also witness to an era inasmuch as its date of erection coincides with the type of house built during the Reformation, in common with others established in the region at this time. Moreover, it is interesting to note that 80 per cent of the wood composing the house could be re-used in its re-erection, and that the building was employed by the Baden-Württemberg Forestry Commission in 1979 to house its Forestry Museum. At the house front a wide door opens out into the feed alley. The cattle were assembled along each side of it, that is, at right angles to the house ridge on the left and right. This fact distinguishes the house from others in the Black Forest. The narrower doors on the same side were for letting the animals in. Immediately behind the main door there is a compartmentalised area for stalling horses. The living quarters of the house are reached via a staircase leading to a narrow hall and the front door. Behind this, the visitor finds himself in the parlour, perhaps taken by surprise by the size of the room and its vaulted ceiling. Again, the focal point of the living room is the ex-

Lorenzenhof. Farmhouse built about 1540 in keeping with the style of the Reformation, a period important for Kinzigtal.

Lorenzenhof. View of the parlour with its table and decorative wall.

*Lorenzenhof.
"Herrgottswinkel" in the parlour.*

tremely decorative **Heergottswinkel,** its column and table as well as the oven area directly opposite, but here with an oven of cast iron. This type of stove is only to be found in the upper Kinzig Valley and its subsidiary valleys. The parlour is furnished in addition to one or two paintings on glass, a cupboard, a chest, two clocks, a number of tablets of religious import, and a little container for holy water. The bedroom is not positioned above the li-

Lorenzenhof. Iron plate from the oven in the parlour.

ving room, but next to it. It is rather smaller in size which is an advantage to the kitchen to be found adjacent and further inside the house. The bedroom, in addition to revealing the usual furniture, also displays a hand organ which once belonged to **Fürst vom Teufelstein,** described by Hansjakob as a "gallant, jolly forester" and hunter who died on the 27th April, 1893. The kitchen, too, presents nothing other than the expected, a relatively modern iron

Lorenzenhof. View into the bedroom adjacent to the parlour.

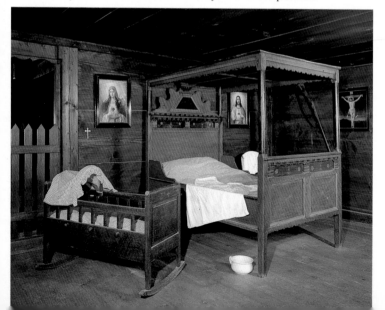

*Lorenzenhof -
kitchen cupboard
with plate rack
and other wooden
untensils.*

cooking range with a number of hotplates and a bar running
round it. The large water pan of course must not be missing in
such a scene. The smoke from this oven was drawn out through
the rather odd-looking flue into the large cowl, from there into
the corridor, over the "smoke shelf" and out into the open air.
The presence of this type of stove indicates of course that even in
old houses owners used modern apparatus. It's the same today
when people live in old houses and wish to preserve them for the
future.

Next to the kitchen we find the children's bedroom. Today, this
has been adapted as a museum exhibition informing the visitor
about glass manufacture and raft-making. The room opposite served as sleeping quarters for the adult daughters of the family while the one to the right of the front door was for maidservants. Today, it houses documentation on the development of mining in
the Black Forest.

Above house and barn in which hay and aftergrass were stored
ranges the attic with its ramp and entrance, and again we find the
"lying chair" roof construction whose angled supports are connected to the roof beams of the so-called "house" while those of
the barn rest on supporting beams which are five-cornered in
cross section.

Since wood and the wood trade was basic to the existence of people living in the Black Forest right up into the 19th century, it
was quite appropriate that the Forestry Commission in Freiburg
should set up a museum in **Lorenzenhof** in 1979. In this section

we see the beginnings of settlement in the Black Forest which, in all probability around the year 1000, consisted of almost untraversible forested hills. As far as commerce with wood was concerned, the main problem was its transportation. The model is of considerable interest as also the exhibits and illustrations on the use of streams and rivers for this purpose. The employment of wood at home is also amply documented, for example, as fuel, as building material, its use in crafts such as that of the lathe-worker, cooper, carpenter, carver, vat-maker, shingler and in boring wood. Wood was also put to use in mining and smelting. It was much sought after in the production of charcoal. Tree trunks provided resins and bark which in their turn could be further processed. The wood itself was also an auxiliary in pasturing since the leaves were used as straw substitute. Clearing woodland leads on then to farming and the role played by the forest in agricultural economy past and present. Finally, one is introduced to the present plight of our forest and to its vital functions for us humans, as a conserver of water, as protection against avalanche, wind and a regulator of local climate, as a place of work and also of recreation, as nature reserve and living space for rare animals. The exhi-

Lorenzenhof. Room used either for servants, the daughter of the house or for elderly members of the family.

69

Lorenzenhof. Various implements used in rafting.

bition should be regarded as an appeal to consistently take care of forest land and to use it sensibly and thoughtfully.

As already indicated, before the coming of the railway and the lorry, the transport of wood was a considerable problem, and so streams and rivers were extensively employed. For this reason, the making of rafts belongs to one of the oldest trades in the region. The loggers and raftmen were frequently members of associations like those of earlier guilds. One thinks, for example, of the Association of Murg Boatmen and the Wolfacher Boatmen's Association or the Schenkenzeller Raftmen's Team. Trade and rafting went hand in hand and Black Forest logs were transported as far as Holland in assisting shipbuilding there. Then came the railway and the end of rafting.

Wood was indispensable to the glass industry. At one time it was needed to reduce it to potash in several operations. And, of course, one required wood to heat the smelting ovens. For the production of one kilogramme of glass about 1-2 cubic metres of wood were needed. This in turn required the felling of large areas of woodland in the neighbourhood of of glass manufacturers, for example, in both the north and south of the Black Forest. The glassmakers themselves were much sought after as specialised craftsmen and so they wandered from place to place. Because of this we find families of the same name in St. Blasien or in Gengenbach. The glassmaking tradition as glass-blowing reached its zenith in Offenburg and Achern prior to the introduction of modern industrial techniques. After the First World War, however, glass-blo-

Lorenzenhof. Equipment used in glass-blowing. This was an ancient and important trade in the Black Forest.

wing in the old manner was set up again in Wolfach and continues today.

At one time, glass-blowers, their assistants and many craftsmen in glass were also farmers. They used their fields and gardens very intensively because of this and we can see just how this was done at the Museum in the garden of **Lorenzhof**. Here, we are concerned not so much with variety as with economy. In other respects,

Flails used in threshing.

the farmer's garden was much the same as the monastery garden or those of the castle and the mansion. It was near the main building and was usually square or rectangular. Paths were either laid with stones for the main part or bark chips. The latter kept pests away. Individual plant beds were surrounded with boxtree about eight to ten inches high. The garden as a rule contained sections for spices and for flowers, another section for herbs an the largest section was reserved for useful plants and vegetables. Small fruit trees or fruit-bearing bushes were a rarity. These were usually to be found within the farm's orchard. Generally, the garden was fenced with a paling, plaited twigs, a hedge, boards or latticework. It was felt that a museum garden should also be pleasing to the eye since, after all, plants have been prized and tended for centuries, and for that reason they are worth restoring to our gardens and accepting within our lives again today. With this in mind, the herb garden behind **Vogtsbauernhof** was considerably extended in 1984. It now contains almost a hundred different kinds of herbs and poisonous plants to be found in the Black Forest region.

Farmers' garden near Lorenzenhof, here an example of an intensively cultivated garden not far from the main building.

A shrine set up in the year 1747 ⑲ brings us back to **Lorenzenhof** and rafting. The miniature raft behind the main building, the so-called **"Bähofen"** ㉑, well and post, all these are invaluable objects testifying to rafting and their construction. On the reverse side of the shrine is a representation of a raftman's boot, an indispensable article of clothing in this watery profession. The raft at

Well, twig-heater and post used in the construction of rafts.

Raftman's boot on a wayside post dated 1747 reminds the passer-by of the days of rafting.

the rear of **Lorenzenhof** is a smaller model of a raft with three sections, the one at the head having a rudder, is smaller and more manoeuvrable. On the central section stands a "Stock", a structure to which the raftman tied his clothing and victuals. The raft's last section has a braking mechanism. The function of the **Bähofen** was to soften hazel, ash, willow and pine twigs after which they were wedged into the nearby post and then twisted over one another much in the same way as wire in order to be used as raft binding.

The Kinzig Valley bakehouse ㉒, the upstroke saw ㉓ and the shrine next to these can be seen in a neighbouring building to the **Lorenzenhof**. The bakehouse was set up in 1972. It has a gable roof and stands somewhat removed from the main building for safety reasons. Its function was the same as that for the bakehouse near **Vogtsbauernhof**.

Bakehouse at Lorenzenhof standing some way from other buildings. In the entrance one can see the shelves for finished loaves.

The upward stroke saw was built in 1890 next to **Lorenzenhof** in Urach and transferred here in 1970. It replaced the so-called "thud" or "knock" saw around 1800 and is additionally equipped with a flywheel which enabled the saw to function both on its upward and downward stroke.

A wayside shrine dated 1802 is dedicated to Christ and the Virin.

Drying and crushing hemp ㉔

Hemp cultivation was an essential element in the production of coarse fibres for ropes, but also for finer ones in the manufacture of clothes bed linen and tablecloths, for example, and was carried on over an area which stretched from the Rhine Valley into the foothills and central highlands of the Black Forest. Seed was set in May and harvesting took place in August. Afterwards, the stalk was allowed either to stand in the meadow to rot or was placed in so-called "Rötzen". The material was then then exposed to the sun, put in an oven or dried in special kilns so that the fibres deta-

The hemp pounder rendered the fibres pliable and smooth. Here, we can see inside the meachnism as far as the first double camshaft.

ched themselves from the stem. Then the hemp was "broken" or hackled. In order to render the fibres soft and pliable for combing and spinning, the fibres were first rubbed or pounded. The hemp-drying kiln on exhibition arrived at the Museum in 1986 and was found at **Vorhunselhof** in Hinterlehengericht. It lay below the farmhouse near a stream in marshy land whose water level was slowly rising. Unfortunately, the oven has not been offcially described since it was not an article of value worth keeping safe. At any rate, we have to do here with a ditch roughly three feet deep which widens conically at its top. Below, a fire burned and dried the hemp stalks on a grid above.

Hemp pounder showing mechanism.

The hemp grinder and barley pounder were brought here from Oberen Mühle in Steinach in 1968. A mechanical grinder of this kind was rarely to be found in a village except as the occasional example. From this we can assume that the farmer had an additional income. The machine itself consisted of a grinding or rubbing bed onto which the hemp was thrown and rubbed and turned. This was a round, sandstone block having a diameter of 2,4 m (approx 7,8 ft). The crushing stone was of granite and roughly conical in shape and ran round the basin, so breaking down the hemp fibres. Water drove the main wooden shaft as in the case of the grain pounder above and this in turn was geared to the shaft of the grinder vertically and horizontally.

Between the grinder and **Leibgedinghaus** we come across another boundary stone with the coats of arms of the House of Württemberg and Falkenstein ㉕ . The latter shows a stag standing on a three-pinnacled hill. The mountain represented lay above the town of Schramberg and belonged to the monastery of Tennenbronn east of Gutach over the mountains.

The boundary stone between Württemberg and Falkenstein. The antlers represent the House of Württemberg.

Leibgedinghaus ㉖

The last building on the Museum tour is Leibgedinghaus, a cottage built for the aging farming couple. Generally speaking, when the farmer reached his sixtieth year he bestowed the farm on his youngest son. If the farmer was rich he could afford to build his own pensioner's house. But this was the exception. The cottage we see was erected in 1652 in Gutach on **Neubauernhof** and re-erected here in 1964. It is also representative of the type of house lived in by smaller farmers, jobbers and tradesmen. From its construction it is a mixture of the Gutach and Kinzig Valley house.

Retired couple's house. This is a mixture of the Gutach and Kinzig Valley type of house. It was also the kind of house occupied by the day labourer.

As a house built level with the ground with its kitchen in a central position it resembles the Gutach house, whereas the vaulted ceiling in the parlour with its "smoke shelf" calls the Kinzig house to mind.

At ground level we find a little parlour, a kitchen and a bedroom all of which are accessible via a corridor running along the long side of the house. A door next to the main entrance leads into the livestock area where there was room only for a few animals. Its layout resembles that of the Kinzig Valley house. The vaulted roof which is some 16 inches (40 cms) below the roof flooring is especially striking. The "Herrgottswinkel" with its rich decora-

Retired couple's house. Parlour with oven an special tiling.

tion suggests that the owner was catholic. The line for spoons with its two examples further suggests that there were only two people occupying the house. The oven with its characteristic tiles is a so-called "Tyrolen stove" may remind us of the great many day labourers who came over the mountains into the Black Forest as mountaineers and tree-fellers. The tile, because of its larger surface area was a more effective reflector of heat. This particular tiled oven or stove was useful for drying socks and hose, to warm apples or pears, even braise them. Other articles of furniture are a chest, a clock, souvenirs of military service, a bird cage, a "God bless this house", a petroleum lamp and a shotgun. This was customary in Harmersbach and was the farmer's right of possession. Next to the parlour is the kitchen and in it is an oven of particular interest since it belongs to the earliest type of transportable oven in the 60's of the last century. The kitchen also has a smoke cowl which stretches right across its length. The bedroom reveals a

Retired couple's house. Kitchen with transportable iron stove.

Retired couple's house. Sketch showing house construction.

four-poster, a wardrobe, a cradle, pictures of saints, a crucifix, a commode, an enamelled clock and a container for holy water. The stalls of the house usually had room for a cow and a goat. The attic is only accessible via a ladder and for that reason cannot be viewed.

Retired couple's house. Bedroom with abundant furnishing.

The smithy and oil mill ㉗

These two commercially lucrative appointments are not in the main part of the outbuildings belonging to a farmhouse, although they are very closely associated with farming life either as places where important apparatus was manufactured or where agricultural products were processed into new products. At the same time, they round off the economic scene in the Black Forest, the smithy's shop especially representing an important connecting link with modern industrialisation. Smithy workshops such as this with its hammer and oil mills were accommodated in stone buildings or half-timbered property. For this reason they are housed in a new building at the Museum which is a replica of a 16th cent. half-timbered workshop. The fact that the two are under one roof is not an anachronism. On the contrary, it confirms historical fact, a fact which can be substantiated by a report on a fire which took place on 25th Feb. 1795 from which we learn that it broke out "in a small building some distance away in the smithy where an oil mill had been installed".

Smithy's shop and oil mill. Here, they are to be found under one roof as was the case in Gutach during the 18th century.

The mechanical hammer in the smithy powered by water and used for the manufacture of hand tools and apparatus.

The most important piece of apparatus is the tail helve or hammer brought to the Museum from Ottenhöfen. It consists of a double-armed lever which swings in one direction. The one end is connected to the axletree or a water wheel via a camwheel which raises and lowers the beam. On the other end is the hammer itself which strikes a steel, mounted base plate. It was used to manufacture small iron tools such as axes, prong hoes, picks, hammers, locks and ironwork for waggons. The farmer needed these every day. Iron could be wrought by heating it on the hearth nearby with the help of the bellows. Finer work could be carried out on the anvil and on the work bench. Hammers, pliers punches and bosses were essential in in such work. Apart from the making of light tools it was also the smithy's job to shoe the farmers' horses and not only to shoe them, but also make the shoes themselves. In addition, he put the iron bands round apple-juice and wine barrels as well as washing vats. These had often to be widened or narrowed or adapted in some way. We can see the tools used in this work on the nearer wall. The iron itself was supplied by the nearby ironworks.

In the broader, central valley of the Black Forest favoured by good climatic conditions, rape, flax, beechnuts, nuts and poppy were planted and harvested. From these oil could be obtained which was not only used for human consumption, but also as fuel for lamps. This oil was provided by the oil mill. The one we see was brought here in 1974 from Bickelsberg near Balingen. It has a crushing mechanism activated by water power. The mechanism

The oil mill crushed rape, flax, beechnuts, nuts and poppy for oil to be used either as lamp oil or food.

itself is a vertical wheel which revolves in a rill and is later pressed out by the press to the left. The oven we can see was used to extract linseed oil by watering it down and then heating the crushed seeds.

Behind the mill building there is a small pond which offers plants and wildlife a natural place to thrive.

Everyday life on the land

Touring the Museum has no doubt given the visitor some insight into life as it was lived on the land. A few generalities might be mentioned here. The farmers occupying the houses were, up to

The construction above the well was used to cool milk, butter and other foodstaffs.

the 19th century, feudal tenants in subservience to their lords spiritual and temporal. They did not own the farm as their property, but were obliged to pay tithes and dues to those who owned the land. It was only the French Revolution and its consequences which made it possible for he farmer to purchase land and farm at a high price from his landlords. Then as now, the work of the far-

The cream from milk was turned and beaten in the butter vat until butter solidified from it.

Cowbells. The bell named "A Paris" recalls cattle droves as far as Paris.

mer was concerned with his fields, meadows and woods in the main, while his wife looked after the house, garden and livestock. The daily routine lasted from 5 o' clock in the morning until 9 o' clock at night. After a soup in the morning, there were sandwiches about mid-morning, then midday meal followed by a bite to eat during the afternoon from a knapsack and then a soup again in the evening. The midday meal consisted for the most part of potatoes, farinaceous food, vegetables, sauerkraut and fruit. Meat was rare before 1900. The soups were compounded of milk or water and in the best case from meat as a broth with bread, flour potatoes and ground cereal. Herbs and vegetables were planted by the farmer's wife in the garden which was near the house. Vegetables were so planted that about the middle of the year there was always something to harvest. Grain crops and potatoes were cultivated on the fields. Meadow land as well as pasture brought in hay and aftergrass, and here both were at work. The strenuous work in the woods was a man's job, but it's probable that his wife and children lent a helping hand in this. Wood sledges were indispensable during this work. From time immemorial, the keeping of livestock was basic to existence on a farm in the Black Forest. It was necessary for the production of milk, butter, fat and leather. Above all in the morning and evening, tending the animals took up a good deal of time. Also very important was the well supplying water for man and beast. This was to be found either inside or outside the house and there, too, one had to wash. The well housing served as a "refrigerator". The family found their peace in the parlour which was the only heated room in the house.

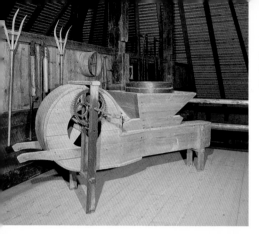

This mill was responsible for separating chaff from grain mechanically.

The berry press crushed fruit to obtain their juice. Bilberry wine was also produced in this way.

As soon as fruit cultivation was possible, the farmer distilled his own spirits.

The farmer as artisan

Today, living as we do in an age of specialisation, it may appear a little odd that practically every trade had its origin at the farm. Because of the remoteness in those days of the farms, bad roads, constant exposure to the whims of the weather, especially during the long winters, the farmer was all too frequently thrown back on his own resources. The presence, for example, of a hand-carved chair in practically every farmhouse is proof of the fact that the farmer himself was capable of making his own tools and apparatus. Some of these skills sufficed to make him an independent artisan. One thinks of the wood-carvers, the spoon-makers, the coopers, broom and brush-makers and also the watchmakers. This last developed in the first half of the 17th century in the neighbourhood of St. Märgen and St. Georgen. In the early days one only required a knife, a saw and files. Since 1700 the Black Forest clock has been an important article of trade. Wood-sawing and the grinding of corn also grew up in the farmer's sphere of activities, activities which the farmer undertook himself until the 19th century. The interior layout of a house required the skills of

The tailor and the seamstress would visit the farmhouse to make clothes for men and women.

the so-called "applecart men", the shoemaker, the carpenter, tailor and basket-maker. The wood taken from the forests in itself a hard, specialised task was responsible for the development of a number trades connected with its processing. One recalls the work of the raftmen and lumbermen, the charcoal burners, the potash extractors, the ironworkers and glass-blowers as well as

The cobbler repaired shoes for everyone at the farm. New shoes were made in his own workshop.

the shingle-maker. His work consisted of first cutting blocks about fifty centimetres (roughly 2 ft.) high from pine or fir, splitting these into triangular, smaller blocks before making them into wooden tiles. These were then smoothed and were afterwards ready for the roof where, according to the age of the tree, they would remain for the next 25 to 50 years. However, the shingle-maker was not wholly concerned with the manufacture of roofing tiles. He also prepared beechwood chipping rich in resin for burning in simple lamps which preceded the oil and the petroleum lamp, and was contemporary with the candle, supplying the principal source of illumination in the parlours of those days.

One used to say that the high point in a farmer's life was the erection of his house, a job in which about 40 to 60 people took part at a time when there was not much to do in the fields and one that

had to be accomplished as quickly as possible. The necessary joiners were, after all, rooted in farming life. The carpenter or joiner was a competent man and one who enjoyed considerable esteem, for it was his responsibility to see to it that the house was built securely from good material to withstand the vagaries of the climate. And so it is not for nothing that his name often appears along with the owner's over the front door.

Carpenter's tools are versatile;wood and iron were the principal components.

Piety among the people

One of the aspects of life among the people of the Black Forest can also be followed up in the Gutach Museum. Their religious attitudes both towards the church and in the worldly sense were characterized by a mixture of heathen and Christian teaching and experience. Added to these were factors associated with natural phenomena and the seasons. One thinks of the secular cults of **Fastnacht** and Santa Claus as well as the custom of protecting the

"Herrgottswinkel" in Hippenseppenhof is adorned with a madonna in the corner column, has glass paintings and other religious depictions as well as a rosary and dove of the Holy Ghost.

house by magic involving and being determined by both moral and Christian considerations. The many crosses along the way, for example, though having received the blessing of the church, were almost certainly also inspired by ancient, pagan ideas of driving away evil. They plea for God's support, result from vows and

*For the old people in the Leibgeding-
haus or cottage, the Herrgottswinkel
is also a place to retire to.*

*Above the altar at the farm's
chapel, four patron saints are
to be seen: St. Andrew, Simon,
John the Baptist and St. Anthony.*

pledges, recall family events or are oracles of warning. The same
can be said for the shrines, a selection of which we have already
seen in the Museum. The hallway cross from Hotzenwald carries
both a warning and a reflection. The "Longinuskreuz" on **Hippenseppenhof** could just as well stand in the hall. Chapels near
the farmhouse were primarily places for prayer and devotion often came into being as the result of a vow or religious inspiration.
For domestic devotions there was the "Herrgottswinkel" with its
crucifix flowers, rosary and madonna.

Around this, in the corner formed by the column and window,
were religious pictures, partly in the form of glass painting and
partly as prints ranged along the wall. Then followed, close to the
table, pictures of lords and princes, military souvenirs and photographs of the family. In protestant families icons and crucifix were
replaced by the family Bible. The abundance of religious pictures
is lacking and was replaced by patriotic material. The prayer for
help and protection in the "Herrgottswinkel", in the farm's chapel, before the wayside cross and the shrine was intensified by receiving the sacraments and by pilgrimage. Thus, baptism, first

communion and marriage brought a good many customs with them. The customs affecting death come to mind as well as those associated with All Saints Day and All Souls. Famous places of pilgrimage such as St. Märgen, Friedensweiler, Todtmoos and Zell, the many votive pictures and gifts at those churches indicate how strong the clamour for saintly guidance and succour was and how varied the distress was in the daily lives of those who sought assistance and libertion in need God and His saints.

Nevertheless, this marked Christian piety didn't hinder the people of the Black Forest from clinging to their pagan customs, sayings and symbols. The fear of ghosts and spirits was very widespread. These were said sometimes to sit on a man's chest or on his back and in this way to bring him to the ground. Above all, it was felt necessary to keep evil away from the animals and so one kept a billy-goat near the stall to hold the witches at bay. The farmer felt no qualms about having the sign of the Three Kings above the front door while the next door was adorned with a lucky horseshoe and a broom to drive away the evil ones. Even the "Herrgottswinkel" was decorated with a horseshoe and, on finishing the roof timbering, the draft animal that had brought the wood was slain and its skull hung up on the first post supporting the ridgepole. Thus, house and family were assured that no harm would befall them.

The Longinus Cross showing instruments of torture also depicts this Roman soldier riding towards Christ.

Glass paintings going back to the 18th century are witnes to the artistic activity of Black Forest folk.

Regional Costumes

The frontispiece of this brochure shows **Vogtsbauernhof** as the nucleus and namesake of the Gutach Museum. It also shows the ceremonial costume which belong to it, not for the sake of cheap effect, but to underline the significance of the Museum's region. This Gutach costume, then, does not signify the Black Forest for which it is often mistaken and commercially misused for touristic purposes. In reality, the **Gutach Tracht** as it is called is unique to only three villages and represents a very small area (Gutach, Kirnbach and Reichenbach) in comparison with other regional costumes. It is possible that the consequences of popular art, photography, music and early tourism have led to the **Gutach Tracht** being identified with the Black Forest and even internationally as a symbol for West Germany in general.

The theme of regional costume has in fact a direct reference to the Museum in Gutach. On the other hand, no attempt is being made here to enter into competition with the Black Forest Regional Costume Museum in nearby Haslach. While the latter exhibits and documents all the numerous costumes in all their variety, the Gutach costume can only be mentioned and demonstrated as simply a component of farming life in association with the Museum's houses. It is only possible to allude to the problems involved with regard to national costumes here in a short, general way since it is felt that the whole history and development of the **Tracht** must be completely re-written. For there is hardly another area which is so subject to ideological misinterpretation and false representation as the problem of regional costume. Not so long ago, for example, the Hotzenwald costume was displayed as the oldest because, so it was said, the Hotzenwald folk had allegedly brought back their wide breeches from Spain after returning from war. After all, these wide-fitting trousers had long been known as "Hotze". However, we know today that this garment was the general wear for farmers in the late Middle Ages. Most recent research has shown that the word "Hotze" is also the name given to a particular linen woven in Hotzenwald. These examples merely to show how careful one must be in dealing with the subject. One can, however, say that farmers' dress from the end of the 17th cent. to the middle of the 19th was the result of regulations as to what should be worn and laws determining this laid down by regional overlords. Fashion as well as artistic skill are aspects that also play a part. These have affected various articles of apparel in regional costume as, for example, the different hats of straw. The five farms represented at the Museum display five different costumes: the Hotzenwald, the High Black Forest Costume for the Schauinsland Hou-

The Hotzenwald regional costume.

The Münstertaler Tracht shown here belong to the Schauinsland area.

The Furtwanger Tracht belongs to the Hippenseppenhof.

The occupants of the Lorenzenhof were clothed according to the House of Fürstenberg.

The "bulb hat" regional costume is confined to only three villages, viz. Gutach, Kirnbach and Reichenbach and not to the whole of the Black Forest as people suppose.

se, the Furtwanger Tracht for **Hippenseppenhof**, the Gutacher Tracht for **Vogtsbauernhof** and the Fürstenberger Tracht for **Lorenzenhof**. All these regional costumes are documented. The woman wearing the Fürstenberger Tracht, for example, wears white stockings, a variously coloured flowered skirt, a colourful bodice with a short jacket, a large flowery silk neckerchief as well as a beret on unmarried women and a pointed cap on married women. The most important attribute for Gutach women's regional costume is the bulb hat, the little bonnet, the velvet shawl with coloured edges, a bodice of black velvet with woven-in flowers, the socalled "Wifelrock", a skirt stretching to the calves with a black silk apron and white stocking woven of hare fibre. The men's costumes of these neighbouring regions are similar in that they wear a long, black kilt which is lined with red inside. The black, broadbrimmed hat is also similar. The Fürstenberg man wears a waistcoat of flowered velvet, silk knee breeches and white or blue stockings.